whiskey words & a shovel II

whiskey words & a shovel II

r.h. Sin

Andrews McMeel
PUBLISHING®

absence and peace.

your absence taught me

how to live without you

time away taught me

to find peace

in being alone

human flaw.

we hide behind the human
condition

of making mistakes

using imperfection as an excuse

to hurt those who love us

expecting things to go back

to how they once were

after apologizing

reminders.

you kill your future

by mourning the past

sin's request II.

I want to undress her soul

and feel her aura against my
own

I'd like to get to know the things

deep within her

my eyes have already grown
familiar with her physique

I'd like for her to undress her
soul

and allow the universe inside

of her to speak

I welcome the moments

where I can literally

taste her aura

those moments where my
own soul

can explore her

exits.

ex is short

for exit

this is what I've come

to realize

stop leaving the door
open

for someone

who no longer

deserves a key

tangled.

how quickly we become twisted

tied and tangled

within each other

lost in a translation

that only we can comprehend

I understand your complex

emotions

flowing, crashing like waves

within the ocean

open for me to enter

so good, I refuse to leave

we get each other

we know exactly

what the other needs

best revenge.

I remember that feeling

the cold air dancing on my
hands as they were the only
thing to be exposed

I sat there on the balcony of the
apartment we shared

I took a deep breath and yet this
heaviness remained sitting
within my chest

it was in that moment that I'd do
anything to watch you crawl in
pain

it was in that moment that I'd do
anything to make you feel the
way I did

but then I realized that the best
revenge would be to become
more of everything you failed to
appreciate, everything you'd
one day search for after the
world had its way with you

and when you returned

I'd be gone

enjoying myself, happy and
peaceful with someone stronger
than you were

the search.

I set out in search of love and
what I often found was chaos
and destruction

hearts filled with malice and
souls that resemble winter

eyes that wander and lips that
lie

I set out in search of everything
that I could've given myself and
I know that now

all lies.

they were all lies, she thought to
herself while picking up the
pieces of her own heart

silence, my friend.

I've been hurting and I can't
find the words to explain what I
truly feel

and if I could

I don't believe you'd be able to
comprehend the words within
my soul

this is why I say nothing

as if silence is my only friend

encouragement I.

stop teaching women how to
think like men, we rarely think

don't encourage her to become
the very thing that continues to
destroy her

don't encourage the type of
behavior that makes men appear
weak

encourage women to be more of
who they were meant to be

respectable, valuable, loving,
and strong

intelligent and beautiful

encourage her to be the type of
woman that sends weak men
running the other way

a war with self.

it's difficult

it's been painful

it's been weighing you down

you know it's time to let go

you know you deserve more

you know he's not who he used
to be

blinded by love

your emotions betray you

every time

it's the constant battle

between

what you know

and how you feel

fantasies.

she's an angel

with a filthy mind

early December II.

I remember thinking that I'd
never get to speak to you again
and so I wanted to tell you every
single thing that I could

for the first time in my life, I
wanted to be completely
transparent

and even though you were just a
stranger, you felt so familiar

I didn't know you but I knew
you from somewhere

maybe another time, a time
where most of our conversations
were pillow talk

or most of our interaction was in
the midst of silence, lying
awake, late nights

afraid to sleep because that
would mean temporarily leaving
one another

I don't know, I just wanted to
tell you everything

everything that you missed
while being distracted by
someone who wasn't me

everything you missed while in
the arms of someone who didn't
deserve to hold you

everything you missed while
confessing your love to
someone who failed to
reciprocate the things you
expressed

that night, early December

read closely.

you miss the person you thought
he was

you're in love with everything

he used to be

you hold on because your love
is unconditional

you're up, thinking about him

wanting his attention

maybe a text, a call, maybe you
just want to lay up and cuddle

but he's always doing this

he's rarely around and it hurts

that's what keeps you up at
night

you're hurting right now and
he's probably asleep

understand this

life is too short to lose sleep
over a living nightmare

I know you love him but you
have to love yourself more

see, anyone not willing to
respect what you feel

is not worthy of any type of
emotional response

how many tomorrows will you
spend waiting for a man who
only deserves a place in your
yesterdays

your future is uncertain because
your focus is on your rearview
mirror

you can't get to where you need to
be

focused on everything that
belongs behind you

long distance.

I'd kill the distance
to get to you

tainted love II.

you spoke of love

but there was hatred in your
actions

you spoke of love

and yet all I felt was pain

you spoke of love

until I stopped listening to what
turned out to be a lie

in the form of everything I
wanted to hear

11:50 p.m.

it's hard, it's always been
difficult

but I just think we're
looking for the type of love

that doesn't destroy us in the
end

the type of love that helps us
evolve and grow

it's important to realize that this
type of love is only attainable

once self-love is achieved

rare.

love is rare

heartache is too common

sadly, searching for love

often leads to more heartache

enough.

you can't keep blaming yourself
for someone's inability to be the
type of mate you deserve

I used to do that often

lost in my own feelings

made to feel as if my all wasn't
good enough

when really

I had the terrible habit of falling
for those who weren't good
enough for me

because I was unaware of my
own value

cracks.

here you are covered

in cracks from falling

and not being caught

cracks from loving

someone incapable

of reciprocating everything

you gave them

and yet here you stand

still beautiful

still worthy of the love

you've always given

I wrote this for you

flames.

you felt like hell but I stayed
there

in flames for a love that never
did exist

in flames for a love

you weren't capable of giving

broken beautiful.

she was quiet
but her silence screamed
her silence told a story
where words often failed

her heart like winter
dry air upon her lips
as she exhaled
after taking in
all she'd been through

broken yet stronger
hurt but wiser
a few cracks in her foundation
and still
she remained beautiful . . .

love 722.

you drive me mad
but make me laugh
imperfect, our love
but perfect for me

losing to gain.

we lose things to gain more and
sometimes what we lose isn't a
loss

in time, your heart will heal

in time, your heart will be ready
once more but only for someone
who is ready for you

masks II.

what I wanted was the most

honest parts of your soul

and what I received

was everything I tried

my hardest to avoid

people wear masks

too large to fit

and in time

you begin to realize

that the face you see

isn't really theirs

in between sleep.

my mind knows what my heart
continues to ignore

I'm tired but I can't find sleep

lost, between the hours of 1 a.m.
and 3

restless under the same moon as
you

eyes, the truth.

smiling with sad eyes

I've seen what you've

been hiding

after 3.

it's after 3 a.m.
and I can't sleep
my mind won't quiet down
and my soul can't help
but wander

lying here, still
appearing peaceful
but there's chaos
deep within me
struggling to close my eyes

a smile.

I don't remember the time

where a smile actually meant
happiness

sadly, so many of my peers

only smile to hide things

encouragement II.

stop teaching women how to
find a good man

and start encouraging them to be
the type of women that no-good
men can't even approach

memories.

be careful who you make your
memories with

love and lies.

your detailed text messages

his one-worded response

you make yourself available

but he never finds the time

you're always calling first

he refuses to call at all

but you're stuck

because you fell

he claimed to love you

but in fact he didn't fall

still learning love.

I'm still learning about love

and what it means

to physically share myself

with someone who cares

for my heart

and my soul

I'm still learning about the type
of intimacy

only shared between two people

destined to be a part of each
other's life

I'm still learning how to touch
and how to feel

I sometimes struggle with

the emotional side of it all

because I've only known

to remain unattached

after the act

nightmares.

and you were a nightmare
wrapped in something beautiful
a disaster presented as a gift

different, yet the same.

different person

same pain

different person

same lies

I hate the moments between
meeting someone and leaving
someone

there's this brief feeling of trust
before the paranoia that seeps in

once you begin to realize that
they're just like everyone else
you've met before

different person

same bullshit

resolutions.

changing for the better

ready for something better

reality.

you're unhappy

you've been feeling neglected

you've been taken for granted

and yet you still find ways and
or create several excuses as to why
you stay

in reality

you've been holding on

to nothing

so if in this moment

you decided to walk away

you'd lose them

and at the same time

you'd lose nothing

you'd gain peace

you'd lose them

yet find yourself

be there.

I don't want to be this way

I hate the way this feels

sometimes I just want to quit

sometimes I refuse to stop

I'm all over the place

and I just need you to be there

oh, broken soul.

you're a mess

you've been broken

you're guarded

you have baggage but I'm not
afraid to stand beside you

I'm willing to help carry
whatever it is

that may be dragging you down

I'm willing to climb the wall
you've built

I love you for who you are

even when you think your soul
isn't good enough to reap the
benefits of my love

falling short.

you weren't strong enough to
catch me

and that's fine

you weren't brave enough to
love me and that's okay

I forgive you for failing at
pretending to be everything

that I wanted

I forgive you for falling short

of my expectations

the unforgettable.

you're unforgettable

women like you don't

come around often

your presence is

electrifying

not for the weak of heart

maybe that's why he couldn't

keep you

maybe he just wasn't strong

enough to hold you

know that whomever you are

wherever you are

there is someone searching

for a love like yours

the Lexington.

I thought I knew the sound
of love
until it was delivered
in your voice

I thought I knew what it felt like
until your hands touched
my own

that early evening
in midtown Manhattan
I thought I knew passion
until it happened
when we kissed
I felt love, a bit of lust
I felt your skin
and I felt this

this tingle in my spine

the relief in my chest

you made me moan

you made me grow

you took away a life of stress

and somehow

everything I thought I knew

was within you

the whole time . . .

my scars.

these scars

remind me that I survived

everything meant to

destroy me

sleep.

you know what's painful

sleep is no longer a means of
rest

it's something most of us do in
order to forget the things that
tear us up emotionally

something that most fail to
achieve

lying there wide awake

drowning in an ocean of their
own thoughts

we're all the same

we're all seeking relief

Natasha's interlude.

you were so young

yet so strong

an unmovable force

even in the uncertainty of your
own life

you made certain to instill hope

in those closest to your heart

you played many roles

in your youth

and you'll continue to

so as a tribute

to everything you've been

and all that you'll become

to the big sister I never had

to the mother of a son

the wife of a soldier

and the daughter to a King

I love you

on most nights.

you're in love, heartbroken or
both

lying there restless

watching the night bleed into
the morning

wishing you had more hours to
rest

your mistakes.

don't beat yourself up

for being too good

for them

don't be so hard on yourself

for choosing someone

incapable of appreciating

everything that you are

sometimes you have to

choose badly

in order

to be able to identify

what is good for you

release.

sometimes crying means

letting go

sometimes the only way

to empty yourself of a person

is to shed tears

often pretending.

sometimes it hurts

to be strong

sometimes it hurts

to be the one who
seemingly

never needs help

drowning in your

own emotions

pretending to enjoy

the rain

while hoping

for more sunshine

good-byes.

this here is the end, my
departure, my good-bye

wanted to stay

pushed me away

but I'll be fine because I tried

see, you'll wake up and regret it

didn't give me enough credit

I was throwing several hints

it's a shame you didn't catch it

you'll wake up

try to call

but nothing is what you'll get

time's up, no more chances

walked away, this is it

the blueprint.

just be good to her
remain loyal to her loyalty
and reciprocate her love

forget not.

never forget the people who
made you feel as if your best
wasn't good enough

never forget the way they
mistreated you while you gave
them what was considered your
all

remember their faces and ignore
that I miss you

I'm sorry and I love you

when you've walked away for
good

most nights.

in a dark room

my mind's lit

a dark dreary soul

cold in search

of the type of warmth

that only can be found

on a half-made bed

between the legs of a lover

who knows my pain

mentally fatigued

from giving a fuck

feeling stuck in a place

where caring drains the soul

and on this night

I'd like to feel nothing

but sweat running down my
chest

pressed against a lover

who knows my pain

I just want to feel at ease

as the breeze

from that old dusty-ass fan
blows

my mind so far in the gutter

dirty from thoughts of you

as I begin to grow

and I just want a lover

who knows

how it feels to feel like me

potential.

in love with your potential
suffering from the reality

my mind knows
what my heart ignores

easily forgotten.

I don't have exes

just a few mistakes

a list of regrets

and things gone up in flames

from the bridges I've burned

love that felt more like pain

and truth that turned out to be
lies

I don't have exes

just a few individuals

that pretended to be more than
they were

individuals who fell short of
something appealing

I don't have exes

just a few people

who were easily forgotten

soul relatable.

and to the women

who wake up tired emotionally

restless during the night

unable to sleep

drained both physically and
mentally

smiling in an effort to hold back
the tears

you are beautiful

you are good enough

you are strong

you are survivors

3:33 p.m.

they only treat you

how they feel

about themselves

tired.

I just want to know love

like I know hate

I just want a love

similar to my own

often off, my emotional switch.

I've always given myself in
small doses and sometimes
nothing at all

careful not to share the best
parts of myself with someone
who could turn out to be the
wrong person

protective in terms of my heart
and soul

understanding that most of the
people I meet will fall short of
my expectations

and so I've learned to expect
nothing

sometimes my emotional switch
remains off

you can't get hurt if you feel
nothing

survival.

you can't force something to be
more than what it should

sometimes the people we love

can't comprehend what we feel

and there will be times where
you'll have to walk away from
the very person whom you'd do
anything for

it's not giving up

it's simply survival

and I hope it's you who survives

drown.

overwhelmed by a sea of
emotions

sometimes you have to drown

to learn how to swim

used to it.

I was so used to being hurt
that I continued to allow you
the opportunity to destroy me

I'd walk away, only to return
giving you permission to burn
through the foundation
that once represented us

in flames
I learned the lesson of settling
for someone
who had grown comfortable
with breaking my heart

encouragement III.

stop teaching these women how
to deal with no-good men and
motivate them to avoid these
types of men altogether

teach them self-esteem and self-
assurance

teach them self-love and respect

on my way text.

roses blooming

the sun setting behind the ocean

rain gently falling upon my skin

head rubs and light kisses on my
neck

hands clasped, refusing to let go

lavender fragrance

a slightly cool breeze

these are things you make me
feel

everything that you are is
everything that I need

I love you

I know when your heart is
heavy or when you're stressed
or when your mind is all over
the place

I'll take you away

when I come home.

broken but magic.

there's still magic in a heart
that's been broken

oceanus.

our souls became the ocean

immediately crashing against

each other

so wet as we collided only

to become one

forced together by nature

this mix of you and I

was supposed to happen

diving into love

emerging within each other

sunsets then rise.

she was the sun

the way she fell

into the night but managed to
rise every morning

brighter than before

masks III.

and that's what it always boils
down to

you meet someone

they're everything you wanted

you fall

only to discover their true self

you're in love with a mask

and even after that mask is
removed

you hang on to the possibility of
that person wearing that mask
once more

essentially, becoming the person
you fell in love with

no judgment, I get it

I understand, I've been there

I know how difficult it can be

the restlessness that follows the
act of falling for the wrong
person

the aftermath of realizing that
your love was only conjured up
by a false representation of what
you thought you needed

but losing something fraudulent

makes room for something real

guarantees.

being a good man or woman
doesn't guarantee you true love

loving someone

doesn't make them the one

seasoned love.

I don't want puppy love

I now require something
seasoned

something stronger

straight like my favorite liquor

I want something

homegrown from seeds

within my soul

watered with truth

and loyalty

I'm not a child

and I no longer have the need

for childish things

give me imperfect

but give me your best

I want your love

in its purest form

I want you

sadly.

sadly, one of the hardest
loves to find is the love
your heart deserves

yes, you.

you deserve to be someone's
only choice

emotional CPR.

we try our hardest to force life
into things that must die and
that's what hurts the most

in search of heaven.

love doesn't feel pure anymore

it's become all about what we
can do for each other in terms of
physical pleasure and often
defined by material

I can't say that I miss it

the way it used to be

because whatever it's been

I've never had the opportunity
to claim it, to have it, to hold it

and that's the story most of our
hearts tell

searching for a love that
resembles heaven

yet somehow we end up in hell

stubbornness.

your heart is stubborn

sadly, it clings to the things

that break it in hopes

that those things will save it

one day.

one day you're going to regret
hurting her heart

one day you're going to regret
destroying the woman with a
heart that deserved to be loved

and your regret will always
come at a moment too late

for once her heart is completely
shattered

she'll learn to pick up the pieces
without you

forgiveness.

I'm still trying to forgive myself

for all the things I failed to
become

I'm still trying to make peace

with all the broken pieces of my
past

self-blame.

passing the single mother in the
grocery line as she looks over at
the magazines with a tagline
that reads

how to keep a man

as she begins to base her self-
value on whether or not she can
keep men interested

a thought occurred to me

maybe it's not her

maybe it's not her at all

maybe it's her choices

choosing men who just don't fit
into the plans of her future

maybe we should write more
articles that help encourage self-
love instead of self-blame

maybe that's the cure

maybe self-love leads to
choosing a man capable

of reciprocating everything

she's willing to share

harsh reality.

it hurts to watch the person you
love

become everything you should
avoid

it's difficult to watch the person
you love

treat you as if they hate you

and even though it hurts like
hell

you continue to hold on to who
they were

instead of accepting what
they've become

it's the harsh reality of falling in
love with the surface

and unexpectedly having to face
the truth in who most people
really are

exes.

I should just change my number

my friends tell me that I should
just block you

I should send you to voice mail
but I don't

I held on to you, hoping
something would change and I
guess this is my way of forcing
you to feel what I felt

hoping I'll answer your call

hoping for something that'll
never happen

good vibes only.

give silence to negativity

understand that those who wish

to harm you in any way

and or disrupt your peace

don't deserve the energy

it takes to respond

to their actions

you're valuable

stop engaging with those

who can't afford you

after hours.

no matter how painful

being alone may actually feel

nothing hurts more

than lying next

to someone each night yet
restless

because it feels as if

you're sleeping alone

strength.

truth is

you're not okay

but you will be

you'll hold on

but you'll let go

it'll be difficult

but you'll do it

you're feeling weak

but be strong

one hell of a woman.

she couldn't be tamed,
rebellious lover

refusing to settle for less than
she deserved

there's this fire that burns within
her

the type which could never be
put out as she used it to light her
own path

she, unchained and free, willing
to push the envelope and rip it
open if she had to

strong in every sense of the
word

valuable even when others fail
to notice

one hell of a woman to fall for

one hell of a woman indeed

sent, text message.

you either be consistent

or become nonexistent

painful truth.

I've come to realize

that those who smile the most

usually shed the most tears

in secret

and those who laugh the
hardest

are usually the ones who cry the
loudest

in silence.

I want to tell you all the things

that sit unexpressed within my
heart

but I'm afraid

you won't be able to
comprehend

my love and so I remain silent

hawaii 722.

I think your love is as vast

as the ocean

and you've been with men

who feared your waves

but I'm not afraid to try

to dive

to taste

to face

the future soaking in your love

past loves.

you have this perception of love

that is false

you talk about it, you write
about it

as for the stories you tell
yourself are all fiction

you pretend to know what it is
or how it feels

when you know nothing of its
touch

you loved the idea of something

they could never give you

yet you fool your heart

into thinking they deserved

a place there

you keep fooling yourself into
thinking that chaos is passion
and that somehow the
destruction of your heart in the
process of loving the wrong
person was beautiful

those past loves were all lies

2013.

a life spent

with someone who constantly

hurts you

is like death

from womb to tomb

some people spend most

of their lives

either surviving heartache

or dying from the weight

of emotional distress

shit, I just want to love

and live while doing so

unchanged.

I think a woman's heart

is made of something

out of this world

as much as it's been broken

she survives

as much as it's been broken

the value of her love

goes unchanged

this is what I realized

while looking into the eyes

of the woman who fell for me

despite a past of having her
heart

mishandled and broken

she trusted me

she trusted me enough

to fall into my arms

the rules.

respect her mind

feed her soul

protect her peace

guard her heart

she became.

your eyes became stars and
what used to be your body

became the galaxy

which is now a place I wish to
live

I'd like to be inside of you

lost with no gravity

traveling within every part of
you

tired of new beginnings but I'm
willing to start with you

over and gone.

unfortunately for you

I won't be standing

where you left me

and you won't be able

to text me "I miss you"

when you finally

become bored with

the person you left me
for

I no longer seek closure

no more bitterness

and my heart is no
longer cold

for I have found the
love

you were incapable of
providing

and I have found
warmth

in the arms of someone
better

interlude for the survivor.

the pain means you're alive

the scars mean

you've always survived

misinterpreted love.

I don't know, maybe I thought
or believed the words you
whispered on that foggy
morning in the nude lying next
to me wearing nothing but my
arms as I held you after we
become one in a moment that
felt like forever. Those words
felt like life as I lay there
slightly drained as I used up
whatever energy I had in trying
to please you.

Maybe I thought that those three
words would extend the
moments that we've
already experienced with each
other. You uttered them to me
with ease without a speech,
simply straight to the point,
making it easier to comprehend.
Now as I sit here with just a
memory of how it was, I
realize that those three words
meant nothing to you but
everything to me.

love of self.

you belong to you

sometimes your soul mate

is yourself

and everything

you've been searching for

can be found

deep within your own soul

a time of love.

thank you for seeing
the stars within my soul
when all I saw was pain
scars and darkness

always worthy.

marry the woman they say is
broken

remind her that no matter how
hurt she may be

she's still worthy of the type of
love that can move mountains

and when she shows you the
scars that have been left upon
her heart by the things scattered
within her past

kiss each one of them and
remind her

that despite it all

despite what she's gone through

she's still the most beautiful
woman in your eyes

words and actions.

saying I want something real

while holding on to something

with someone

who continuously lets me down

someone who constantly

makes love feel painful

someone inconsiderate

selfish and negative

I've been saying I want true
love

while holding on to something

with someone toxic

unsupportive, unreliable

incapable of telling the truth

so much tension, arguments

all this verbal abuse

saying I want one thing

while accepting the opposite

too much.

too tired to sleep

too hurt to start over

too depressed to say a word

I've been there

it gets better

just give it time

an outdated love.

you're in love

with how you remember them

not with who they've become

you're in love with

an outdated version of how
things were

you're attached to an idea

that no longer exists

this is what happens

when those we usually avoid

pretend to be everything

we've always wanted

too late.

no one misses you until you
walk away

no one appreciates you until
you're gone

no one understands this until
you've given up on waiting for
things to get better

no one listens until silence is the
only thing left

encouragement IV.

instead of teaching women how
to keep a man

let's encourage them to be the
greatest thing to and for
themselves

a woman's value is not
validated by her ability to attract
and or keep a man

loveless.

loveless relationships

cause people to love less

that's the problem

with being hurt

you avoid love

altogether out of fear

of more hurt

heavy heart.

every day

a war zone

you're constantly fighting

for your own sanity

in search of peace

smiling instead of crying

laughing instead of breaking
down

you deserve a break

this night is yours

tonight your heavy heart

deserves the light

moving on.

I walked away
I moved on
not out of hatred for you
but for love of self

the more you respect yourself
the less likely you are
to hold on to someone
who fails to appreciate you

people deciding to not show up
is the reason
I decide to go missing

no freedom.

there's no freedom in loving the
wrong person

you spend most nights, locked
away in your own mind

overthinking and driving
yourself mad

to love the wrong person is hell
on earth, death in life

an emotional prison

fraudulent emotions.

most people find themselves

in love with the person

who is keeping them

from finding true love

sadly, we've become a
generation

content with being in love

with a love that isn't real

hell here.

hell on earth will always be
trying to maintain a relationship
with someone who is too weak
to remain loyal to the idea of a
forever with you

women like you.

and she just sat there

cold but beautiful

broken but deserving

so much chaos in her soul

but still in search for peace

I think every woman with a past

just wants a future

where everything is different

better than what they've known

I think women with a wall up

are at times

the ones who love the hardest

and it's women like that

I find the most attractive

flaws and all

there's still magic in her eyes

cracked, sometimes shattered

but there's still value

within her heart

and still.

your heart is fractured but it's
still valuable

awake.

but sometimes

nightmares occur

while we're awake

and sometimes those nightmares

come in the form

of those we love

loyal.

I'm too loyal

to myself

to entertain anyone

who can't remain loyal to me

together but alone.

I think the worst time to feel

as if you're alone

is when you're standing

next to the person

you love

and that's the reality

for so many people

being taken

but feeling single

in love alone

gallows.

your past lingered

like a rope around your neck

and so I kicked over the chair

beneath your feet

winter Marie.

grasping at her skin, eager for
entry

somewhere deep, somewhere
warm, away from the cold

I took her and then I wore her
out like a jacket in the winter

the lesson.

not everyone you love

will stay

not everyone you trust

will be loyal

some people only exist

as examples of what to avoid

her interlude.

and there she was

lying there alone

eyes fixated on this page

this book

these words

her emotional mind state
unknown

but I knew

and I wrote this for her

I wrote this for you

you're going to be fine

why we stay.

that's the problem

instead of using our strength

to let go

we'd rather hold on

to what was

ignore what it's become

while destroying

what it should've been

we want so badly to be loved

by those filled with hatred

we continuously search for
peace

where only chaos lives

self-care.

betrayal makes the heart fragile

handle yourself with care

the emptiness.

you just get so damn empty

sharing yourself for the sake of
keeping them interested

giving them your all and yet
they act as if it's nothing

she is you III.

and I could still hear her heart
breaking

the eerie silence

followed by a soul cry that was
so loud

it could have awakened

her ancestors

a pain so deep that not even the
ocean could match its depth

waves of disappointment and
lies

forgiveness, second chances, and
betrayal

would drown her in that
moment

I witnessed that as I hung my
head

wishing there was something
that I could do

my arms stretched open but
she'd never see them

point of view blocked by
someone she loved

the very person who deserved
none of her heart

I witnessed her heart shatter into
a million pieces as I struggled to
watch

but even after all of that

even after the tears drowned
whatever joy she had left

she found the strength to pick
up the pieces and that was truly
beautiful

she is strong, she is you

Tati's interlude.

this is for all the thank-yous

you deserve but rarely get

this is for all the moments

when you grow tired of the
bullshit

this is for the drama

that looks for you

this is for anything, anyone,

or anybody who plans on
stressing you

may they continue to fail

or fall beneath you

where they belong

there is strength

beneath your surface

there is love in your heart

and there is patience

in your soul

you are and will forever remain

stronger than the things

or those who come against you

comparisons.

I compared her to the moon

because even in darkness

she remained beautiful

I compared her to a sunrise

because I'd awake before her

to witness the opening of her
eyes

January 28th.

for me, love has always been
like winter

it comes and goes

whiskey wordplay II.

eyes swell

telling a tale

of hell and chaos

souls looking to collide

with another

but left alone

with a slow song of sadness

the madness of searching for
something beautiful

in a scene filled with destruction

and pain

it always rains for those

longing for the sun

craving change in terms of love

but so often it ends the same

and as exhausting as it is

we're all looking for the same
damn thing

no chance.

ask yourself

why you miss me

and you'll understand

why I'll never let you back in

weaknesses.

their inability to remain faithful
to your loyalty

is a reflection of their own
emotional handicap

and has nothing to do with you

stop blaming yourself for their
weaknesses

and start preserving your energy
for someone who is strong
enough to reciprocate the love
within your heart

keep in mind.

sometimes the devil promises us
a piece of heaven

sometimes darkness

disguises itself as light

be careful, be strong, be wise

lack of love for self.

they hurt you

and you think nothing of it

they hurt you

and you try harder

they hurt you

and you apologize

they hurt you because

they don't love themselves

self-harm.

loving the wrong person is self-
harm

the future.

I hope something real

finds your heart

I hope your heart discovers

the truth about the type

of love that you deserve

cracks in foundation.

we're always stitching together
the good things

we're always stitching together
the moments of peace and joy

that's why it's harder to let go

that's why it's harder to move
on despite the chaos that
plagues our soul

we'd rather remember the good
and suppress the bad

we see cracks in the wall, in the
foundation of everything we've
built and instead of demolishing
this weak structure of a
relationship

we paint over, gloss over, and
try to rebuild what no longer
deserves our energy

we.

we run out of second chances

we get tired of excuses

we get tired of being taken for
granted

we get tired of arguing

we get tired of making an effort

we get tired of losing sleep

we get tired of entertaining the
bull

even good people with big
hearts

who love hard have their limits

not love.

we see chaos

we feel pain

we know loneliness

and yet

we call it love

burial.

unhealthy relationships are dead
things

waiting to be buried

we fall.

. . . but that's the thing

we fall in love with untrue
versions of others

we continue to fall

failing to realize their
unwillingness to fall

beside us

then hang on

for dear life

in hopes of things changing

they rarely do

they almost never do

the wrong lover.

constantly, we find ourselves
torn

between holding on to the
possibilities of change

and realizing that what we
hoped for was just a dream sold
by yet another soul too cold to
make good on empty promises
and a love that never actually
existed

I know that feeling all too well

stuck under the spell of brown
eyes and lips that lie

but failing to realize the signs

until it's too late

and that's the fate we all suffer

in terms of choosing the wrong
lover, I've been there . . .

the journey.

the path toward peace

is filled with chaos

tough is the journey

but the destination

is worth it

decisions.

you can't help who you love
but you do decide
who has the potential
to be loved by you

nothing.

it's going to hurt like hell

you'll have days

where your peace will be
compromised

your heart will be tested

and you'll feel as if you're
losing the one you love

but is it really a loss

if the one you leave behind

did nothing to make you stay

avoidance.

you are rare

I mean

there's something

inside you

that can't be found elsewhere

avoid anyone who treats you

like you're ordinary

avoid anyone incapable

of seeing what

you've always seen

in yourself

warrior heart.

she has the mind-set

of royalty

and the heart

of a warrior

she is everything

all at once and too much

for anyone who

doesn't deserve her

she is you

she's always been you

deserving.

she wasn't being needy

she was simply in
search

of everything she
deserved

choosing yourself.

walking away

doesn't mean you stop caring

for those you've distanced

yourself from

sometimes you come to the
realization

that it's time to take care

of you and sometimes

that means leaving

behind people

who stopped giving a damn

about you

the woman.

I've been searching for you

the woman with a past

deserving of a better future

the woman who knows

how it feels to have her

heart broken

left alone to piece

herself back together

the woman with the type of love

that most men fail to
comprehend

the woman who knows

the true meaning of loneliness

betrayal and deceit

that woman deserves to be loved

and I'd like to be the one

to reciprocate what she's

been brave enough to share

you are not your past

and I'd like to be a part

of your future

that fear.

the fear of not being good
enough makes you try harder
for those

who aren't good enough for
you

be patient.

if you're brave enough to let it
die

you'll find new life

in something beautiful

with someone

willing to treat you better

and the patience

you've invested

into the wrong people

is just enough

to preserve your heart

for the one who deserves it

at this moment.

you miss the way he was when
you first met him

you fell in love with everything
he pretended to be

you won't let go because you're
waiting for things to change

you're reading this now and this
is exactly what you needed

I'm not judging you for staying
but I do want you to know

that you deserve so much more

conflict of the heart.

I wanted you to come back

but didn't want you to come
back

that's what hurts the most

wanting something

that has proven to be toxic

magic.

one day someone will look at
you with magic in their eyes
because that's what you are

emotional reaction.

more and more I'm learning

that I have complete control

over my reaction to the actions

of others

and I refuse to allow myself

to provide an emotional reaction

to those who are not worthy

of my energy

I refuse to be broken

by those who have always

been too weak to stand beside me

I refuse to be torn down

by those who sit below me

now.

it's time to take the love he
could never appreciate and give
it to yourself

thank you, the end.

dear woman, thank you

thank you for being brave
enough to love

thank you for being brave
enough to try once more

even when that love goes
unnoticed

thank you for smiling through
the pain

thank you for the strength
that you've displayed

may your will to survive be the
inspiration for this piece

in this moment

you are my muse

thank you

index.

whiskey words & a shovel II

Andrews McMeel Publishing
a division of Andrews McMeel Universal
1130 Walnut Street, Kansas City, Missouri 64106

www.andrewsmcmeel.com

17 18 19 20 21 RR2 10 9 8 7 6 5

ISBN: 978-1-4494-8035-6

Library of Congress Control Number: 2016934683

Editor: Patty Rice

Designer, Art Director: Diane Marsh

Production Manager: Cliff Koehler

Production Editor: Erika Kuster

attention: schools and businesses

Andrews McMeel books are available at
quantity discounts with bulk purchase for
educational, business, or sales promotional
use. For information, please e-mail the Andrews
McMeel Publishing Special Sales Department:
specialsales@amuniversal.com.